MULANI MONEYBAGS' ABC'S OF BUSINESS

by Kelly Wallace and Mulani Ellington

Mulani Moneybags' ABC's of Business

Copyright © 2021

by Kelly Wallace and Mulani Ellington

All rights reserved

No part of this book
may be reproduced or used in any
manner without written permission of the
copyright owner except as permitted by
U.S. copyright law.

For more information:
info@ilemonbk.com
P.O. Box 50328
Brooklyn, NY 11205

FIRST EDITION
ISBN: 978-1-7366168-3-3

www.ilemonbk.com

Table of Contents

A: Audience
B: Boss
C: Cost
D: Demand
E: Entrepreneur
F: Features
G: Goals
H: Help
I: Idea
J: Job
K: Kiosk
L: Loss
M: Mentor
N: Networking
O: Opportunity
P: Profit
Q: Quality
R: Referrals
S: Sales
T: Teamwork
U: Under-promise (AND overdeliver)
V: Value
W: Wholesale
X: eXceptional customer service
Y: Yes
Z: ZZZ's

If you want to be a successful **_entrepreneur_** like me, all you have to do is follow my ABC's of business! Are you ready? Here we go...

Aa

A - is for **_audience_**.
The people you decide to sell your product to, are called your **_audience_**. Will other boys and girls buy your things? Or do you want to sell your products to their parents?

Once you've made that decision, you will have an easier time finding them. When you get your product in front of your **_audience_**, they are more likely to buy it from you if you think about what they want. Then they will go from being your **_audience_** to being your customers.

My **_audience_** is everyone who loves a delicious, cold, homemade lemonade on a hot, sunny day.

Who is your **_audience_**?

_____
_____
_____
_____
_____

Bb

B - is for **_boss_**.
When you own your own business, you are the **_boss_**.
Being the **_boss_** comes with many responsibilities.
The **_boss_** is in charge of making all of the decisions.
The decisions that the **_boss_** makes, determines if the business will succeed or fail.

As the **boss** of my business, I had to decide what my lemonade would taste like. If it didn't taste good and people didn't like it, my business would not be successful.

Do you think you are ready to be a **boss**?

_____
_____
_____
_____

Cc

C - is for **cost**.
Before you decide to sell anything, you must first know how much everything will **cost**. **Cost** is the amount of money that you have to spend to create your product. In order to have a successful business, you have to sell your products for more money than it **costs** to buy them.

My lemonade has a lot of ingredients that make it taste so good. Before I can sell my lemonade, I have to first buy the lemons, sugar, fruit, ice, cups and straws. Then I have to use my math skills to add up the _cost_ of each ingredient to get the total _cost_. When I go to sell my lemonade, my _goal_ is to sell it for more than what all of the ingredients combined, _cost_.

How much does it _**cost**_ to make your product? How much should you sell your product for?

_____
_____
_____
_____

Dd

D - is for _**demand**_.
Making sure that people need, or even want the product you're selling is called _**demand**_. If people don't need or want what you're selling, they won't buy it and your business won't be successful.

My lemonade tastes great all year round, but it is especially in _**demand**_ during the summertime. People love having ice-cold refreshing lemonade on hot days, so my business does very well during this time.

When will your product be most in _**demand**_ for your _**audience**_?

_____
_____
_____
_____
_____

Ee

E - is for _entrepreneur._
An _entrepreneur_ is a person who starts a business. These people take a risk by spending their money on their _idea_ first, and with hard work, hope to make a lot of money back after they sell their product.

I wanted to be an *entrepreneur* because I love making products that people really enjoy, and I also want to be a millionaire.

Why do you want to be an *entrepreneur*?

_____
_____
_____
_____

Ff

F - is for **_features_**.
Features are the little things that make your product different and stand out from other products that may be similar to yours.

Everyone knows that there are hundreds, maybe even thousands of different lemonades being sold. But some **_features_** of my lemonade are that it is homemade with a special recipe that me and my mom created. I even add fresh, tasty, organic fruits to it. So even though there are lots of other lemonades out there, there isn't one quite like mine.

What are some _**features**_ you can add to your product to make it stand out and different from other products that are similar to yours?

_____
_____
_____
_____

Gg

G - is for <u>*goals*</u>.
<u>*Goals*</u> are <u>*ideas*</u> that you set in your mind of what you want the real-life future result to be. <u>*Goals help*</u> you to stay focused so that you can measure what is working well in your business and what areas need improvement. Without <u>*goals*</u>, it will take you longer to have a successful business.

Before I went out to sell my lemonade for the very first time, I had one _**goal**_. My _**goal**_ was to sell out all my lemonade. No matter how long it took, I wanted to make sure it was all gone before we went home. And because I didn't give up, I was able to achieve my _**goal**_ within two hours.

Write down the _**goal(s)**_ you have for your business.

_____
_____
_____
_____

Hh

H - is for _help._
Help means to offer something that will make it easier for someone else to do something. Your _audience_ wants your product to _help_ them achieve their _goals._ The more people you can _help,_ the more successful your business will be.

I _help_ my customers by bringing them delicious, cold lemonade on hot sunny days. I come to them, satisfy their thirst and they don't even have to wait in line at the store. And when they're done drinking their delicious lemonade, they get to eat the fruit as a healthy snack.

How will your product _help_ your _audience_?

_____
_____
_____
_____

Ii

I - is for _**idea**_.
An _**idea**_ is an inspired thought that can be turned into a product that you can sell in exchange for money. This is the very, very, very first step of any business. You have to come up with an _**idea**_ for a product that you can make at a low _**cost**_ and sell for much more.

My _idea_ to sell lemonade came from a book that my mom gave me when I was eight. From that one thought, I bought the ingredients to make my lemonade at a low _cost_ and then I went out and sold it to my _audience_ for a higher price.

What product _ideas_ can you think of to sell in your business?

_____
_____
_____
_____
_____

Jj

J - is for _**job**_.
A _**job**_ is a task that you are responsible for doing, over and over and over again. As an _**entrepreneur**_, it is your _**job**_ to make sure that your business is successful. Every day, you have to make sure that your product is made well and that your customers are always happy.

As the _boss_ in my business, I have many _jobs_. Some of my responsibilities are to _help_ make the lemonade, put stickers on all of the cups and to tell everyone that I can about my delicious product.

What _job_ do you think you will have to do when you start your business?

_____
_____
_____
_____

Kk

K - is for _kiosk_.
A _kiosk_ is a small, temporary booth area where you can sell your product. As a new _entrepreneur_ you're going to have to be able to show off your product, so that your _audience_ can see it and know that they can buy it from you. A _kiosk_ can help your _audience_ find you and your amazing product.

When I sold my lemonade, I turned a picnic table in the park into a _kiosk_. I setup my tablecloth, cups, lemonade, fruit and ice, and I let my _audience_ know that I had a great product for _sale_ with a big, bright, bold sign.

Where will you set up your _kiosk_ so that your _audience_ can find you?

_____
_____
_____
_____

Ll

L - is for *loss*.

Remember when I said before that *entrepreneurs* take risks by spending their money and hope that they make more money by selling their product in the future? Well, if an *entrepreneur* doesn't reach that *goal* of making more money than they spent, that is a *loss*. As an *entrepreneur* you want to always make MORE money than you SPEND. You do this by buying the materials for your product at a low *cost* and then selling them for a higher price. If you follow this formula, you can avoid any *loss* and your business will be a success.

Before I actually sold any of my lemonade, my business was at a _loss_. My mom had already spent money on all of the ingredients and materials. She took a risk but knew that if we met our _goal_ to sell all the lemonade we had, we would make more money than she spent. Once we began to sell my delicious lemonade, we sold out in two hours, and my business was not at a _loss_ anymore. In fact, we were able to make a nice _profit_.

What are some things you can do to avoid a _loss_ in your business?

_____
_____
_____
_____

Mm

M - is for _mentor_.
A _mentor_ is a person who has more experience doing the same thing you are trying to do. They are a person who you can trust and can give you good business advice because they have done it themselves.

My mom is my main _mentor_, but she also takes me to different events where I can meet other people who have more business experience than both of us. She always gets me new books and shows me other successful _entrepreneurs_, like Mikaila Ulmer, who have done amazing things with their lemonade business.

Who would you want as a _mentor_ in your business?

_____
_____
_____
_____

Nn

N - is for _networking_.
Networking is when _entrepreneurs_ and other businesspeople come together to share _ideas_, interests and information that can _help_ each other. When you _network_, you start to build friendships that can lead to big _opportunities_ for you and your business. _Networking_ can happen at any time, so it's important that you listen, learn and always be nice to people. You never know who can _help_ take your business to the stars.

When my mom took me along with her to speak to the owner of a store in my community to try to get our book sold in their store, they began to _network_. They discussed _ideas_ of how they could _help_ each other reach their business _goals_. Because of them _networking_, we were invited to participate in my first pop-up shop. At that pop-up shop, I sold a whole lot of copies of my first book and was able to _network_ with even more people!

Where can you find some people to _**network**_ with, who can _**help**_ you reach your business _**goals**_?

_____
_____
_____
_____

Oo

O - is for **_opportunity_**.
An **_opportunity_** is a set of events that come together at the same time, that makes it possible for your business to grow. In order to be able to take advantage of an **_opportunity_**, you have to be organized and prepared.

After my mom _**networked**_ with the store owner in my community, the owner gave us an _**opportunity**_ to sell my product to a larger _**audience**_. If we had not been organized enough to be able to explain my business and if we were not prepared with products to sell, we would have missed that _**opportunity**_. But because we were organized and prepared, we were able to take the _**opportunity**_ to make money by selling my products and we were able to _**network**_ with other amazing _**entrepreneurs**_.

What are some steps you can take to be ready for an *__opportunity__* when it comes your way?

_____
_____
_____
_____

Pp

P - is for _profit_.
Profits are the money you have left over AFTER you pay back your _costs_. This is the opposite of _loss_. Remember, the _goal_ in business is to have MORE money after you sell your product, than you spent on making your product.

Using your math skills, you can calculate your _profit_ in three easy steps:

1. First, add up ALL of your _costs_. Be sure not to leave anything out.

2. Next, you add up ALL the money you made after you've sold your products.

3. Lastly, subtract the _costs_ from the money you made after you've sold your products.

The difference that you are left with are your _profits_.

Here is my *profit* breakdown from when I sold my lemonade:

1. Ingredients:

   Water - $0.00
   Sugar - $3.00
   Lemons - $2.00
   Fruit - $6.00
   Ice - $2.00
   Cups - $10.00
   Straws - $3.00

   TOTAL *COST*: $26.00

2. Sold Out I🍋BK Lemonade: $196.00

3. $196.00 - $26.00 = ***$170.00***

What are some ways you can increase your *profits*?

_____
_____
_____
_____

Qq

Q - is for _quality._
Just because the _goal_ of business is to make your product for less than you sell it, does not mean you create cheap, worthless products. Actually, when you are in business you want to do the opposite and create a product that is excellent and of high _quality._ You should always take pride in your product because when you do, your customers will be so thankful that they will keep coming back to you for more. And if your product is of the BEST _quality_, your customers will even give you the highest compliment (and also the next ABC word of business)..._referrals_!

Because there are so many other lemonades to choose from, I make sure that I choose fresh, _**quality**_ ingredients that will allow me to make the best lemonade I can for my _**audience**_. I take care when I am making the lemonade and thoughtfully select the fruit that will go into my customers' cups.

What steps will you take to create a _**quality**_ product for your _**audience**_?

_____
_____
_____
_____

Rr

R - is for **_referrals_**.
A **_referral_** is when your customer tells other people to buy your product because it is of such good **_quality_**. **_Referrals_** are one of the highest compliments your business can get. When your customers **_refer_** your business to other people, it means that you are on the right track.

When I was selling my lemonade in the park, customers would taste my lemonade and then immediately tell other people who were passing by, how good it was. Because I took the time to create a _**quality**_ product, I was rewarded with my customers' _**referrals**_.

How do you plan to get _**referrals**_ from your customers?

_____
_____
_____
_____

Ss

S - is for **_sales_**.
A **_sale_** is a transaction where money is exchanged for the ownership of a product. A business must make **_sales_** in order to be successful. If you don't sell your products, you won't make any **_profits_** and you'll be stuck with **_losses_**.

When I went to sell my lemonade in the park, I was so excited to make my first _sale_. The family bought three lemonades and I still have the first dollar bill I was given from that lemonade _sale_. I had such a good time making _sales_, that I reinvested some of the money to buy more ingredients and materials to make more lemonade.

What will you do when you make your first _sale_?

_____
_____
_____
_____

Tt

T - is for _teamwork._
Teamwork is when a group of people _work_ together using their own individual skills to achieve one _goal._ For a business to be successful, it is important for everyone on your _team_ to _work_ together to make sure that everything runs smoothly.

My _**team**_ is my family, and we _**work**_ together every day to make sure that I🍋BK is the best business it can be. Our _**goal**_ is to make the best lemonade and each person uses their skills to make that happen. My mom is super creative and loves art, so she makes the lemonade look pretty for pictures. My grandma loves to cook and _**helps**_ me perfect my lemonade recipe. My grandpa and uncle are my bodyguards, and they protect me while I'm out selling my lemonade. And me, well, I brainstorm new _**ideas**_ for products and sell, sell, sell. Everyone on my _**team**_ is important and they all _**help**_ my business succeed.

How do the people on your _**team work**_ together to make your business a success?

_____
_____
_____
_____

Uu

U - is for **_under-promise_** (AND overdeliver) You **_under-promise_** when you set your **_audience's_** expectations at a fair level that you know your product can easily meet. However, you don't stop at **_under-promising_**. Once you've set a fair expectation, it is time to "wow" your **_audience_** and overdeliver. This means that you do or give something extra to your **_audience_** that they weren't expecting. This pleasant surprise will thrill and excite your customer and make them so happy with their decision to purchase from you.

When I sell my lemonade, people usually think that I'm just a little girl pouring regular-old lemonade into a cup. But when I present a beautiful, refreshing, homemade, handcrafted, beverage, that is filled with organic fruit and topped with a colorful paper straw, my _**audience**_ is delighted. And when they finally taste it, they _**refer**_ my lemonade to the people around them.

What are some ways you will
under-promise (AND overdeliver) for
your **_audience_**?

_____
_____
_____
_____
_____

Vv

V - is for _**value**_.
**Value** is the fair worth of your product in dollars, based on how useful it is. The more useful and _**help**_ your product can provide to your _**audience**_, the more _**value**_ your product has.

I provide **_value_** to my customers by bringing a cold, delicious beverage to them while they are out enjoying their day. They don't have to stop their fun just to get something good to drink. And when they're done with the lemonade, they have a nice healthy snack to enjoy.

What can you add to your product to give it more **_value_** for your **_audience_**?

_____
_____
_____
_____

Ww

W - is for _wholesale._
When you buy products _wholesale_, that means you buy a large amount of products all at once, for a lower _cost_. This is one way to increase your _profits_, because you won't have to spend as much money on your supplies.

Whenever we can, we buy our supplies _**wholesale**_ for my business. The products that we know we'll use all the time, are usually bought _**wholesale**_. Our cups, straws, and sugar are all bought at _**wholesale**_ prices. By buying these products _**wholesale**_, we are able to save money on the supplies and ingredients we use the most to run our business.

What are some items you can buy for your business at *wholesale* prices to lower your *costs*?

_____

_____

_____

_____

Xx

X - is for _eXceptional customer service._
Now, I know that this doesn't start with an "X", but just stay with me here. _eXceptional customer service_ means that you go above and beyond what your _audience_ expects of you. The _goal_ when you provide _eXceptional customer service_ is to make your _audience_ feel special and appreciated. This will _help_ them have the very best experience with your business and make them want to _refer_ you to their friends and family for next time.

When I am out selling my lemonade, I make sure that I am serving my _**audience**_ with a smile and I always say, "Thank you!", even if they don't buy from me. If anyone has a problem with my lemonade, I do my best to find a solution to their problem right then and there. When you make sure that people know you care about them, they feel good about doing business with you.

How do you plan to provide _**eXceptional customer service**_ to your _audience_?

_____
_____
_____
_____
_____

Yy

Y - is for **_YES!_**
When you start your business, everyone is not going to want to buy what you're selling all the time. It is important to know that people will tell you, "No." But what's even more important is that you keep going in your business until you get a **_"YES!"_** Some people need to think about buying before they actually buy, other people might not have the money to buy, and other people may not need or want to buy what you have for _sale_. For whatever reason you get a "No.", just know that there are hundreds more who will tell you **_"YES!"_** It is your _job_ to never give up!

When I was selling my lemonade in the park, not everyone bought it. Some people didn't want to buy lemonade. Some people don't like lemonade. Some people had something to drink already. Even though I was disappointed after being told, "No.", I would smile, say, "Thank You.", and move on to asking the next person. When it was all over, more people told me "**<u>YES!</u>**", than "No." because I never gave up. And that's one of the most important things that I've learned...you will succeed, if you don't give up!

What are some things you can do to make sure your _**audience**_ says "_**YES!**_" to your product?

_____
_____
_____
_____

Zz

Z - is for <u>*ZZZ's*</u> (sleep)
When you start your business, you're going to be very busy with a lot of <u>*jobs*</u> and responsibilities. But it's very important that you get your <u>*ZZZ's*</u>. You never want to overwork yourself in your business. It's very important to get good proper sleep, so that you can think, work and operate your business to the best of your ability.

After I sold my lemonade for the first time, I was so excited from the day's success that I could hardly sleep. But my mom reminded me that my sleep was important and that I'd have many more _**opportunities**_ to get back out there and sell my lemonade.

How much _**ZZZ's**_ (sleep) do you think you're going to get once you start your business?

_____
_____
_____
_____

Wow, you made it to the end of my ABC's of business. I hope you learned a lot about starting and running your own successful business. I'm so excited that you're going to be an _entrepreneur_ too! I can't wait to hear about what kind of business you decide to start. If you want to share your business journey and keep up with mine, scan this QR code and let's stay connected. Can't wait to see you at the top!

xoxo Mulani

About the Author

Kelly Wallace -

Hi, I'm Mulani's mom, Kelly!

When Mulani came up with the idea to start a lemonade business, I had to figure out a way to teach various business concepts to a young child, in a way that she could understand.

My strategy to teach Mulani about business was the basis for our second book, *Mulani Moneybags' ABC's of Business*. I decided to use Mulani's very own business and everything she had already done as a way to demonstrate all of the sides to running a successful business. I felt that if I could explain it to Mulani, then children everywhere would be able to understand, too.

As a millennial mom, my goal is to teach Mulani important life lessons such as being independent, self-sufficient and success-oriented. With this book, it is my hope that you will learn a thing or two from our experiences, as well.

We're really excited and grateful that you decided to pick up our book and start your own entrepreneurial journey. If you haven't already, be sure to pick up our first book, *Mulani Moneybags Starts A Business* on our website www.ilemonbk.com.

As always, we would love to hear from you! Share your stories, inspirations, pictures, questions, comments, testimonials, and reviews with us at info@ilemonbk.com. Follow us on social media @ilemonbk and tag us to be featured on our page. We look forward to hearing from you!

All the best!
xoxo Kelly

Made in the USA
Middletown, DE
19 December 2021